A gift for

Bill & Marilyn

from

Connie & Scott Peterson

"Because laughter is the best
medicine"

You probably do some things differently now than you did 20 years ago. Well, so do we. We make fun of what is topical, and that changes, so the making-fun-of changes, too. There are things you wore in the mid-'80s that you look at now and you're like, "that's so mid-'80s." Same with jokes. Funny stays funny, but sometimes we look back at topics we made fun of once upon a while back and we're like, "Whoa!" We've learned, we've grown. A little.

Written by Dan Taylor & Shoebox staff writers
Edited by Jeff Morgan & Sarah Tobaben
Editorial Direction: Todd Hafer
Art Direction: Maura Cluthe & Kevin Swanson

Design: Mary Eakin & Christine Taylor
Flip-book Illustration: Renée Andriani
Handwriting: Mary Eakin
Production Art: Dan C. Horton
Cover Design: Maura Cluthe & Christine Taylor

Printed and bound in China

ISBN: 978-1-59530-157-4

Shoebox

Some of the Best

From America's Funniest Card Company

BOK2074

(A tiny little division of Hallmark)

Table of Contents

ForeWord by
William Shakespeare

A ROSE BY ANY OTHER... DRAT!! THESE THINGS ARE TiNY!!

Shakespeare's First Failed Career: Candy-Heart Writer

I've often wondered what I'd be writing if I were alive today. You hear people say, "it's not exactly Shakespeare," whenever something's short and artless, which I guess is kind of a compliment, but were I to put plume to parchment today, what would come of it? Would I be writing greeting cards? Maybe so. They speak to the same kind of emotions and passions that my greatest works did.

Would I be writing Shoebox cards? No. First, they hardly ever use iambic pentameter. Second, they rarely mention Danish politics. Third, well, first and second were really deal breakers for me.

Obviously, I had a flair for comedy. You
don't name a character "Bottom" without chuckling.
And I did jokes about body parts, sure.
And I touched on parents driving you nuts,
kids letting you down, the everyday
frustrations that plague us from the halls
of the castle to the hovels of scullery maids.
Come to think of it, maybe I would write
Shoebox cards. How hard can it be? "Surely,
thou art no longer young!" Hey! Funny!
What'd that take me? A minute? I can drink
coffee and jerk around on the internet
all day as well as the next bard. And
it's a whole lot easier than making everything
fit that stupid ABAB scheme, or whatever.

Yeah! I could be a great Shoebox writer.
If I weren't dead. It's always something.
Ah, well. Enjoy this book. It's not
exactly Shakespeare, but it's pretty good.

William Shakespeare

Pets♡ Unleashed

Who makes a mess on the rug, tears
the leather couch cushion, and licks people
indiscriminately? Right. Your high school
boyfriend. But also cats and dogs.
And cats and dogs have an excuse. Dogs love
unconditionally. Cats, well, cats have strings
attached. But either way, we love them,
we care for them, we make cards about them.

Note: Most Shoebox staffers are
pet owners with dogs beating out cats
by a hair in popularity.

weird threat,
also overheard
in the lunchroom.

Dog   romance

Awww, Look what the cat made for you today!

As gross as this is, ANYTHING a dog could form into a heart shape would only be worse.

If you ever thought too much about all the places in your home your pet has touched with his naked butt, you'd have to move.

Anita

inside:

Hope you find a nice place to eat your cake.

15-POUND CAT IN A
SIZE 5½ SHOE BOX.

Dogs in human situations— Can't get enough of it!

FiFi, A TRUE FRIEND, ALWAYS WARNED MARIE WHEN SHE HAD LINT ON HER BUTT FROM SCOOTING THE CARPET.

An Internet Search for poodles was necessary for this drawing since no staff member owns One. we seem to favor mutts.

Written at
a time when
many of us
were buying our
first houses.

Rex buys a home.

Why golden retrievers don't make good tight ends.

How ironic, that the dog's name is Katowski!

AniMaL INstincTs

If you spoke even a little raccoon, you
wouldn't feel the slightest bit guilty about
making fun of animals. They joke about us all
the time. Right now a bear is doing an
unflattering impression of you getting into
last year's swimsuit. Deer are making
fun of the way you run. Do you think the birds
are picking cars at random?! Face facts.
And laugh right back.

If chickens
bought cards,
they'd be
OFFENDED.

Truly Wrong ⟹

I BOUGHT YOU A STINKING HIPPO CARCASS FOR YOUR BIRTHDAY.

And then I thought,
"Gee, a stinking hippo carcass
isn't a very good birthday gift."
So I'm keeping it in my kitchen
and giving you a card.

inside:

You're getting
the better deal, believe me.
I almost wish
I'd never bought that
stinking hippo carcass.

Might just
qualify as the
weirdest card
we've ever done.

Did you hEAR that, guys? I gEt to go to a big cookout!

If you're Happy
and you know it
CLaMp YOUR HaMs!

Only about ½
the people in
the department
got this. Must
NOT have gone
to summer camp.

Why Don't you read Something, Earl?
Because I Don't Have to go to the Bathroo right now.
Bill W

BOYs will be BOYS

Boys grow into men, but they retain many
of the lovable traits they had when they were
eight. They also retain many of the goofy,
disgusting, and downright frightening traits
they had when they were eight. They may not
do that much growing after all. We'd feel kind
of bad about all the jokes we've done about
men, if not for one thing. They're just
so funny! See for yourself.

Note: An unknown Shoebox artist always
brings, and then leaves, the newspaper in
the bathroom. It is secretly appreciated.

Based on
an actual
3rd
(and final)
date.

New Edible Underwear Designed by Men

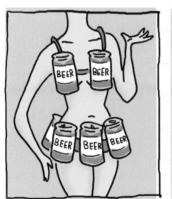
The Six-Pack

The Nacho

Slurpees and Beef Jerky

Please note:
These edible underwear designs **do not** fit in with a low-carb diet.

Led to a **BIG** discussion on why this couldn't work in real life.

Speech bubble: See? There really is a Lake Titicaca!

October 7, 2005

Hallmark Cards
2501 McGee Street
KANSAS CITY, MO 64108

Attention: <u>Whoever is in Charge of Getting the Facts RIGHT!!</u>

Dear Sir/Madam

Enclosed is a photocopy of a Shoebox greeting card which I purchased specifically for my grandson who, at the age of 20, is currently on an extended tour of South America.

I learned about Lake Titicaca and its location in South America (the highest lake in the world) in the 1940's; Kyle (above-mentioned grandson) having actually been on Lake T. can also vouch for its location. However, someone in your firm really goofed when illustrating this card - as you can see, S. America is facing the front while the students are pointing somewhere close to the UK and the other children are looking at Asia!! They are all about as far away from Lake Titicaca as they can get!!

Better be more careful in the future!!

Sincerely

YES, this is an actual letter. And NO, we don't have a Fact-Checking department, because we write JOKES.

HOW A WOMAN SEES IT: HOW A MAN SEES IT:

Sea Spray →  ← GREEN

Garden Moss →  ← GREEN

Very Verde →  ← GREEN

Card inspiration comes from many places, including the Victoria's Secret located near our offices.

Based on the apartment of a writer whose living room consisted of a large screen TV and a recliner.

GiRLS wiLL be GiRLS

The average woman understands that there's no such thing as an average woman. Women communicate at a higher level than men can ever imagine or begin to understand. And that's just when they're talking about hair. Cards written for women are some of the best cards ever because, duh, they're written for the gender that buys most of the cards.

Note: Hard hitting, relevant, empathetic — written, you guessed it, by a guy.

People _love_ this card. Not sure why.

Making fun of guys; Almost _too_ easy.

Also works with:
- Pretend you're a blonde.
- Pretend you're management.
- Pretend you're my kids.

inside:

Pretend you're a man.

Based on a real birthday celebration in the early '90s.

Tami's birthday was ruined when her friends accidentally hired a **real** fireman.

Jan read an article that said you should decorate with things you have lying around the house.

Why is the dog sitting at the table? Extra humor, that's why!

JUDY HAD A SPLIT
PERSONALITY. THE TOP HALF
WAS INTROVERT, THE
BOTTOM WAS NOT.

REViLo

Based on a very funny event that we can't talk about.

Where the Trouble Begins

HUMOR
from
A to DD

Boobs are a big target for humor.
Two big targets, actually. Or small
targets, which is also funny. You can't
do this many jokes shared between women
without getting to boob jokes. Some
of them are written by guys. Guys who are
very scared and very careful not to
make eye contact when the jokes get read.
Here's more than a pair of great ones.

Working staffers'
names into
the cards is
always fun.

inside:

It only took one trip outside
for Sarah to decide that the
boob job was totally worth it.

inside:

Happy Birthday to a woman who hasn't given up hope!

Idea developed (NO PUN) after hearing about an 11-year-old who said something funny along these lines.

Madge thought the new "gravity-defying bra" went a bit too far.

Another bra joke written by a guy.

YOU COULDN'T FIND BETTER BOOBS THAN THESE? AND WHERE'D YOU GET THIS RIVER BARGE OF A BUTT?

THE BRIDE OF FRANKENSTEIN LODGES HER COMPLAINTS.

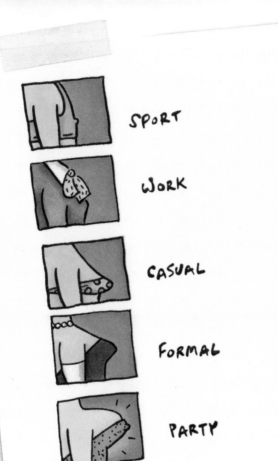

SPORT

WORK

CASUAL

FORMAL

PARTY

cleland

inside:

IF WOMEN COULD CHANGE
THEIR BOOBS AS EASILY
AS THEIR HAIRSTYLES.

RETIRED

shoebox lore:
In 1991, the
average bra
size in the U.S.
was 34B. Today
it's 36C.

Has been read on a reality TV show when it was a cast member's birthday.

inside:

*Your brains and your pride.
(What did you think I was
gonna say?)*

The "Customers" in this card bear a striking resemblance to two of our artists. We've been told it's only a coincidence.

BUTT SERIOUSLY, FOLKS

Butts are funny. You know it's true.
Think about butts for a minute and see
if you don't smirk. If your own butt doesn't
make you laugh, someone else's will. And
if your own butt doesn't make you laugh,
it might make you cry. So there you have it.
Butts cover the spectrum of human emotion.
How could we not do several, and by several,
we mean a lot, of cards about them.

This cartoon was based on a writer overhearing a woman on a subway in chicago say that a celebrity had <u>more</u> <u>cleavage</u> in her <u>boobs than</u> the woman did in her <u>butt.</u> It was immediately translated into a card.

¡Pedro!

Unfortunately, when Madge wished for cleavage, she neglected to specify where.

if books had butts, they would look like this. ⟹

There have been two women named **LIZ** in Shoebox over the years.

No comment beyond that.

we're still
not exactly
sure why
butts crack
people up.

> In any right triangle, the square of the length of the hypotenuse is equal to the sum of the squares of the length of the legs.

inside:

Just wanted to send you
a wisecrack on your
40th birthday.

Plumber Birthday Parties

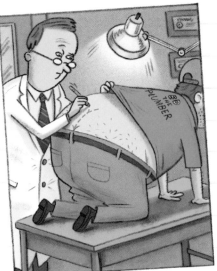

Cosmetic Surgery for Plumbers

Plumbers are the ~~butt~~ of many jokes.

Some jokes are so irresistible, we do them over and over.

This is based
on an actual
ongoing debate
between two
shoebox employees.
No one really wins
this kind of
debate.

It's your birthday.
My butt's bigger.

As long as you show a DONKEY, you can say whatever you want.

Christmas Eve, as seen by Santa

The old saying, "Unless you're the lead dog, the view never changes" reapplied to a Christmas card.

Laughing Burns Calories

At any one time, 30% of the Shoebox
staff are on a diet. Another 30% are
planning a diet. 39% have just ended
a diet, and sworn to just give up and
never diet again. And 1% is the new girl
on the art staff who said she could just
"eat whatever she wanted and not gain
a pound!" She may have said something
after that, but she's dead
to us, so we can't hear her.

Back off, pal.

This idea came to the artist when his own dog had to wear the "CONE OF SHAME" during allergy season.

It's the latest thing. It's called the veterinarian diet.

inside:

You put a couple
of grapefruits
in your sweater
and everything
seems a lot
more proportional.

GUESS WHAT?

The artist of this Card is said to base his drawings on real people. So if you see a guy with a sketchpad looking at you... run.

Chairs from the shoebox break room.

REViLo

inside:

I'VE FOUND THIS
GREAT NEW DIET
THAT REALLY WORKS!

SO WHAT'S NEW
WITH YOU?

Whew! Just taking a break from polishing the silver and planning a week of gourmet meals to say hi before running to yoga class!

You don't want to know what "polishing the SILVER" is code for.

inside:

Right. And then I'm going to Jupiter, because I am their queen! Tomorrow, we invade the Planet of the Apes. Wish us luck!

Two classics...
People love
to hate
themselves.

I gotta buy some
lighter underwear.

HuMoR
OuTLet

"ONE SIZE FITS ALL" is maybe the most cruel
and mean-spirited phrase ever printed,
except when it comes to these cards. Because
shopping is something we take seriously. And
like everything that gets taken seriously,
that makes it a great target for jokes.
Jokes like these. Have a look, but remember,
if you break one, you bought it.

Note: Cartoon inspired by the disturbing
stat that 25% of all women's underwear
purchases are thongs.

Funny
because
it's true.

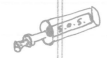

"Shop class" wasn't quite what Tina had expected.

Author Bill Bryson has this to say about our national obsession with shopping—"We used to build civilizations. Now we build shopping malls."

inside:

Clean living paid off,
and Leslie ended up going to Heaven.

People who say you can never have too many shoes have never had three.

Voices Only Women Can Hear

ONLy TeasiNg

We are obsessed with hair. We wish we had
more in some places and less in others.
We want straight hair to be curly and curly
hair to be straight. We think it's funny when
someone loses his hair, and even funnier when
he finds it on his back. Just remember that
no one with so-called "perfect" hair is
really happy on the inside. Sure they may
look happy, but there's more to life than the
outside of the package. All the same, if you
could recommend a good conditioner....

Note: Her word balloon was re-written
like 7 times. The writer is still
not 100% happy with it.

inside:

You've reached the age
where shopping
for hair products
means going to the
sunscreen aisle.

Individual hairs
are one of
the hardest
things for
an artist
to render.

inside:

40... it's not just a skirmish,
it's war.

The tip of the blonde joke iceberg.

Surprise birthday parties for blondes.

inside:

GRAY HAIRS DON'T
HAPPEN JUST ON
YOUR HEAD.

Do yourself a favor,
STOP thinking
about it.

AGING DISGRACEFULLY

Some people say there is nothing we
can do about aging. These people aren't
in the greeting card business. Because
the people who make cards say, "what about
the joking, the joshing, the poking fun?"
Because we, the people who make cards, don't
just talk about aging, we do something
about it. Something funny.

The success of this card is proof that aging bikers have a sense of humor.
yay aging bikers!

And that land mass over there is called a "stick out" because of the way it sticks out into the water.

inside:

Another year older, another year closer to making up crap.

We got a letter from a woman saying this was the ONLY card she was going to send for the rest of her life.

Try listening to talk radio some very early Saturday morning and you'll actually hear stuff like this.

Hi! First-time caller! Let me say I agree with the last caller about bran. Bran rules! Prunes suck! Love your show...

R.

TALK RADIO FOR PEOPLE YOUR AGE.

Might be based on you if you were dining in a popular restaurant chain on May 8th, 1992. It became a card immediately. So, thank you.

Hazing rituals for people your age.

After writing several million birthday jokes, it gets harder to be objective about what's funny and what's JUST WEIRD. This card walks that fine line.

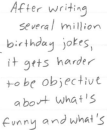

This is one of
those cards that
might seem dirty,
but really isn't.
Or _is_ it...?
(Actually, no,
it isn't. Sorry,)

THE BAD NEWS:

YOUR VISION GETS WORSE AS YOU GET OLDER.

inside:

THE GOOD NEWS:

YOU CAN'T SEE WHAT'S HAPPENING TO YOUR BODY.

One of the artists loses her glasses at least <u>once a day</u>.

The "Missing Glasses" Support Group

BEFORE RUSHING into A FACE-LIFt,
Kim CHECKS OUt HOW iT LOOKS
Oh tHE CAT.

Don't even
act like
you haven't
done this.

THE DWARVES AT 50

Touchy Baldy Squinty

phoot

Gassy Chubby Cranky Drafty

A-A-R-P! I WANNA JOiN THE A-A-R-P-!

THE RETIREMENT VILLAGE PEOPLE

Due to an apparent clerical error, the artist of this card has been on the <u>AARP</u> mailing list since he was about 12.

It ONLY HURTS When I Laugh

Doctors are funny. Nurses are funny. Hospital gowns? Comedy gold! It's almost too bad the average Shoebox fan is so darn healthy because, man, can we make fun of it when they're not! You'll probably want to take our word on this. Read two of these and call us in the morning.

Humor aids in the healing process. Hence, the great ~~popularity~~ of this card.

inside:

They delivered your suppository.

If I were you, I'd get well real soon.

Are you sure you want to fix your trick knee? This is pretty cool.

When old guys dream.

Originally written about glazed donuts, but cheese fries had a better ring to it.

Anita

inside:

Obviously, there are some things insurance won't cover.

Larry's plan to completely cover his bu by wearing the hospital gown backwar proves to have <u>one tiny flaw</u>.

A staff favorite. Well, among the married women anyway.

Hey, look!
It's a
theme!

Not surprisingly, this artist is a mother of <u>three</u>.

Does it concern anyone else out there that this card consistently rates high as a Father's Day card? C'mon Dads. Get a new joke.

Congratulations on your promotion.
I'm sure you earned it.

A HaRd DaY's LaUGh

We work very hard each day at our jobs.
For about 15 minutes. After that, it's
phone calls, e-mails, magazines, seeing if
anyone left anything unmarked in the
refrigerator, and one time, somebody got a
motorcycle and we took pictures of ourselves
sitting on it. But seriously, part of our
work is making cards about work. This is
the kind of thing that, if you really start
thinking about it, can freak you out and
you have to go get some coffee or maybe
just ride the elevator for a while.

This card was actually written on a TUESDAY, but the feeling was the same.

brace

At 3:42 on a ThuRsday afternOon, Ken reaLiZed tHat woRk reaLLy dOes "suCk."

We make fun of bosses, but in private, we _really_ make fun of bosses.

Font on decimal point is Helvetica **Bold.**

"Work is like
one really
long personal
phone call
punctuated by
people wanting
stupid stuff."

– Shoebox writer
   who shall remain
   nameless.

A frighteningly accurate depiction of our booths, except that they are cluttered with collectible action figures.

Butts at the office? GREETING CARD GOLD, BABY!

Relatively funny

We all have family. We refer to them as "the rich soil in which to sow the seeds of humor and then harvest a bounty of jokes." Unless we're in a hurry, then we also call them "family." If you'd like to meet each and every member of yours, just win the lottery. They'll come out of the woodwork! Then you can ask them what they were doing in your woodwork.

Note: Loosely based on a real-life experience of an artist who shall remain unnamed.

HOW PARENTS SEE THEMSELVES.

HOW KIDS SEE THEIR PARENTS!

"The first half
of our lives
is ruined by
our parents, and
the second half
by children."

– Clarence Darrow

Based on an <u>actual</u> sisterly relationship between the writer and her horrible sister.

inside:

Sisters: they grow older, but they never grow up.

When you go into the bathroom and you sit down on a seat that's already warm and it doesn't creep you out, well, that's family.

Ever noticed how in every family there's usually one person who's shockingly normal?

from the shameless self-promotion files:
Hallmark makes cards for over 100 different types of family relationships.

inside:

We should get ourselves one of those.

Written by an
artist who enjoyed
two pregnancies
using this
very tactic.

A fine
example of
the rare,
one-word
cartoon

Ignored her mother's advice.

I do...
What?

Weddings and Anniversaries are beautiful
times. Beautiful for people who make
jokes for a living. We cry, and our tears
are tears of joy. We are also big fans
of the little mints that you can only get
at weddings. Mints of joy. If you would
like to do the Chicken Dance as you read
these, we won't stop you.

Note: More than one happy marriage
owes its existence to another TV
somewhere else in the house.

Words to Avoid If You Write Your Own Vows:

Bodacious
Foxy
Undulating
Whatever
Salami
Bargain
Litigation

The bride + groom cake topper look suspiciously like the artist and her husband.

Renée

Grab all the
happiness you can!

WALLY MISUNDERSTANDS THE
CONCEPT OF TYING CANS TO
THE BRIDE AND GROOM'S CAR.

TOILET HUMOR
WITH REAL
TOILETS!
Quality, cutting-
edge humor.

AS THE YEARS PASSED BY, HERB AND EDNA GREW TO LOOK MORE AND MORE ALIKE.

This card was done by the late, great Bill Bridgeman, a longtime shoebox writer.

Note the
EXCELLENT
PLACEMENT
of the teddy's
ears!

On their anniversary,
Karen greeted David at
the door wearing nothing
but a teddy.

Based on a waiter at an Italian chain restaurant who had aspirations of being a comedian. He's still waiting tables.

inside:

AN ANNIVERSARY TIP: STAY IN, ORDER OUT.

for A SUCCESSFUL Marriage...

Do: Listen to each other and try not to smirk.

Don't: Try to use the remote to mute your spouse.

Do: Spoon in bed together.

Don't: Fork in a public place.

Do: Practice patience and understanding with your spouse.

Don't: Practice voodoo on your spouse.

R.P.K.

Do: Celebrate birthdays
and anniversaries.
Don't: Celebrate arguments you've won
by shouting "In your face!"

Do: Take up a hobby together.
Don't: Take up hatchet
throwing together.

Do: Kiss each other
good night.
Don't: Go to bed angry.
Or in spurs, which
can really rip up
a mattress.

Adults ONLY SEXtion

Sex is funnier than you think. Unless you already think it's funny, then you are right up our alley, so to speak. This is one of those areas where the "corporate sensors" and the urge to be really funny fight. It's a slow-motion fight where a sprinkler unexpectedly goes off and they both get their shirts wet and then they well, you get the picture. Or you can if you have a computer.

Written after a crazy night at a bachelorette party. While the card is funny, the party is still more memorable...

inside:

A girl can dream...

Is it just a coincidence that the author of this card has one AMAZING yard?

Walter found out too late that Helen's secret fantasy had nothing to do with sex.

This card wouldn't have worked had the genders been reversed. As funny as men's secret fantasies may be, they're almost entirely inappropriate to print.

The editor was
EMBARRASSED
when she finally
got the joke.

YESSS!

Judy couldn't stop calling herself
once she got the vibrating pager.

As you grow older, remember-- you can still have the body of a 21-year-old.

This card was written long before <u>Demi Moore</u> made it fashionable to date younger men. Long before.

inside:

First, buy him a couple of drinks...

At our age, kinky sex
takes on a whole new meaning.

The writer of this
card once threw out
her back while
typing (let alone
anything else...)

> "Is it not strange that desire should so many years outlive performance?"
>
> – William Shakespeare
> Henry IV, part 2

WHEN POSSUM WIVES
AREN'T IN THE MOOD

Outings to
the Zoo aren't
just fun and
educational,
they're rife
with card
material!

Madge made a mental note:
Never again on the sofa.

The artist who
turned in this idea
actually owns a bird.
Coincidence?

RaNdom Acts of FuNNy

Humor, by its very nature, is rebellious.
It doesn't fit into your labels and boxes,
man. It wants to be free! Not literally,
but, you know, figuratively. But seriously,
categorizing jokes is tedious, time—
consuming work. So we quit after a while
and just put these here.

The writer actually worked at a lemonade stand in his neighbor's driveway.

When life hands you lemons, make lemonade.

Anita

inside:

But when life hands you a load of crap, don't make anything.

Trust me on this one.

This really happened.

THINGS THAT ARE VAGUELY SCARY:

wigs

taxidermy

public
rest rooms

instant
coffee

The coffee
cup is a
salute to
the many
instant drink
machines
around Hallmark
that dispense
FREE, yet
SCARY
brown liquids.

adults with
stuffed animals
in their cars

Sleep deprivation
techniques are
often used on the
writers to induce
hallucinations
and VOILA,
brilliant cards.

inside:

Ignore life's everyday annoyances
and enjoy YOUR BIRTHDAY!

The artist used his second grade sketchbook for reference.

Maurice's first day as a courtroom sketch artist was also his last.

Less funny
lines we
didn't print:
 - And I
 collect garden
 gnomes

 - And I
 still live with
 my mom.

 - And I
 scream like
 a girl.

One of the
early shoebox
artists rarely
wore a bra.
He really
should have.

If I gave you $10,000 for your birthday, what would you clear, like $7,000? Well, the government's not getting my three thousand, I'll tell you that right now!

stan

A shoebox staffer once won $12,000 in the lottery and didn't even bring in donuts.

inside:

Happy Birthday
(Blame the government.)

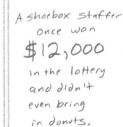

fuNNy, But NO

For every card that ends up in a store,
there are many, many — let's throw in one
more— many that don't make it. Why? Lots
of reasons. Some are obvious, some are
trade secrets that we can't tell you so
quit asking. Read these and see if you can
tell why they never made it to a store.
Some cards are good for laughing, not so
good for sending.

Another year
older and you're
still totally
with it.

So am I, but
in my case,
the "it" is
my husband.

**FUNNY,
but NO.**

Happy Birthday
from the perfect
pair.

And my husband.
(what can I say?
They really are good.)

**FUNNY,
but NO.**

She looked at him
with a look that
seemed to say,
"I'm looking at you
like this because
I want to have
sex with you."

**FUNNY,
but NO.**

Europe, in a
Nutshell:

PROS

CONS

Rich history +
culture

Fat guys in
speedos

CHRISTMAS JUST WOULDN'T BE THE SAME WITHOUT PEANUT BRITTLE.

OR JESUS.

FUNNY, but NO.

It's a drag to find out your card is "funny, but no." But what really sucks is when your card is just "No."

Honey, I wanted to surprise you on Valentine's day.

So I'm leaving you.

Bye

You're like the NBA of the 1980s.

You, too, have a Magic Johnson.

FUNNY, but NO.

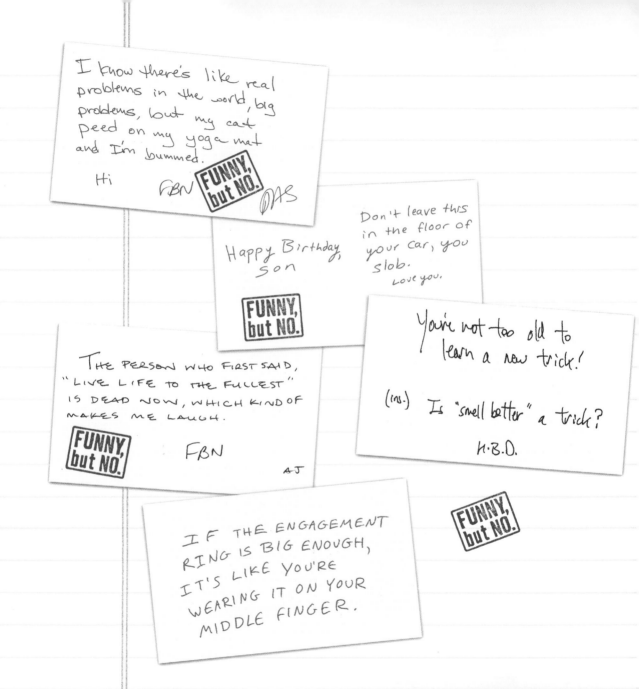

Honey, this Afghan your mom gave us is really warm!

Ahhh. It is YOGA class you seek. Next door you shall find it, yes.

You trigger a kind of protective impulse. I want to shield you from the dangers of our world.

FUNNY, but NO.

EXCEPT for birds that fly right at your head. How creepy are they, with their beaks and talons and the squawking? You're on your own if it's birds. H.B.D.

IVE BEEN WAITING A LONG TIME FOR SOMEONE LIKE YOU. HOW LONG?

FUNNY, but NO.

THEY SAY THAT THERE'S A SOUTH AMERICAN TICK THAT WILL WAIT PATIENTLY ON A TREE LIMB FOR OVER 3 YEARS ~~JUST~~ TO DROP ON THE BACK OF ~~THE~~ JUST THE RIGHT WARTHOG.

THAT TICK IS NOTHING. I SPIT ON THAT TICK. B

SO YOU'RE GETTING A LITTLE OLDER, TRY GOING PLACES YOU'VE NEVER BEEN BEFORE

FUNNY, but NO.

You KNOW, ACT LIKE YOUR HAIR.

HB   AJ

When someone tells me "Into each life some rain must fall!" I like to dump a bucket of water on their head and say "You mean, kind of like that?"

FUNNY, but NO.

Dear Santa Claus,
This iz Billy.
I wanted the RED PowerBot, not the BLUE one!!! Next time, get it right, Stupid!
Love,
Billy

I planned to get you heirloom jewelry for your birthday.

But Grandma rallied. Stupid modern medicine.

Happizzle Valentizzle!

what?

FUNNY, but NO.

Although none of these could ever be cards, they make their way onto a department bulletin board where they live on.

It's your birthday, as the french say, ~~Laissez~~ Le Bon Temp Rouler!" or as we say, "Let the Good Times Roll!"

Hey. Ours sounds better! For once ours sounds better! We win! U.S.A. U.S.A. Happy Birthday P.S. U.S.A.!

When you throw up, you find out that you're not really chewing up your food that well.

FUNNY, but NO.

Try to keep your cake down.

Congrats on your pregnancy!

I pee'd on a stick once. I was in the woods. The results weren't positive.

FUNNY, but NO.

Hey! Need somebody to kind of hit on your fiancé so you can see how he responds? 'Cause I totally will, if you like. I've got an outfit picked out.

FUNNY, but NO.

Here's a fun game — Next time you get pulled over and the cop asks, "Do you know why I stopped you?" Just start listing stuff.

The body in the trunk? The uzzi? My meth lab?

AJ

Another good thing about small towns: Kind'a chunky girls can win the beauty pageant.

Have a small town beautiful birthday,

FUNNY, but NO.

For more funny, but no's, go to www.shoebox.com where we occasionally remember to update the site with new ones.

— Oh, look! Timmy's growing his third ball!

May the holiday wonders never cease.

FUNNY, but NO.

I confused my library card with my sub sandwich card and read 10 books for nothing.

Stupid Jared

FUNNY, but NO.

Shoebox wouldn't be Shoebox without all the people
who have come and gone the past 20 years.
Here's to everyone who has ever helped make
the thousands of Shoebox card ideas a reality.
Our apologies to anyone we missed. Don't be mad.
Although you're cute when you're mad.

Like the book? Let us know!
Didn't like it? Who asked you, anyway?
Book Feedback:
2501 McGee, Mail Drop 215
Kansas City, MO 64108
or email us at booknotes@hallmark.com